IT'S DECORATIVE GOURD SEASON, MOTHERFUCKERS

BY
Colin Nissan

CHRONICLE BOOKS
SAN FRANCISCO

Text originally published by *McSweeney's Internet Tendency* in 2009 (*It's Decorative Gourd Season, Motherfuckers*) and 2015 (*It's Rotting Decorative Gourd Season, Motherfuckers*).

Library of Congress Cataloging-in-Publication Data available.

ISBN 978-1-7972-1366-8

Manufactured in China.

Design by Neil Egan.

IMAGES: **COVER:** © Ali Efe Yilmaz/Shutterstock.com; **1:** © Ulrika Kestere/Offset.com; **2–3:** © Karen Roach/Shutterstock.com; **4:** Zoom Team/Shutterstock.com; **8–9:** © Sam Edwards/Getty Images; **10–11:** © Ziggylives/Shutterstock.com; **12–13:** © iStock.com/skynesher; **14–15:** © AS photostudio/Shutterstock.com; **16–17:** © The Picture Pantry/Offset.com; **18-19:** © iStock.com/SelectStock; **20–21:** © demarcomedia/Shutterstock.com; **22–23:** © iStock.com/Peopleimages; **24–25:** © Smileus/Shutterstock.com; **26–27:** © CaseSensitiveFIlms/Shutterstock.com; **28–29:** © Candace Hartley/Shutterstock.com; **30–31:** © adriaticfoto/Shutterstock.com; **32–33:** © Westend61/Getty Images; **34–35:** © Prostock-Studio/Shutterstock.com; **36–37:** © Izabela Magier/Shutterstock.com; **38–39:** © iStock.com/Ron and Patty Thomas; **40–41:** © iStock.com/FangXiaNuo; **42–43:** © Martin Sepion/Unsplash **46–47:** © Dorothy Merrimon Crawford/Dreamstime.com; **48–49:** © Stakhov Yuriy/Shutterstock.com; **50–51:** © Irina Tkachuk/Shutterstock.com; **52–53:** © iStock.com/Prostock-Studio; **54–55:** © melissamn/Shutterstock.com; **56–57:** © Alexander Oganezov/Shutterstock.com; **58–59:** © Elena Nichizhenova/Shutterstock.com; **60–61:** © BlueLily7/Shutterstock.com; **62–63:** © iStock.com/FatCamera; **BACK COVER:** © Valentina_G/Shutterstock.com

10 9 8 7 6 5 4 3 2 1

Chronicle books and gifts are available at special quantity discounts to corporations, professional associations, literary programs, and other organizations. For details and discount information, please contact our premiums department at corporatesales@chroniclebooks.com or at 1-800-759-0190.

Chronicle Books LLC
680 Second Street
San Francisco, California 94107
www.chroniclebooks.com

It's decorative gourd season,
motherfuckers.

I don't know about you, but I can't wait to get my hands on some fucking gourds and arrange them in a horn-shaped basket on my dining room table.

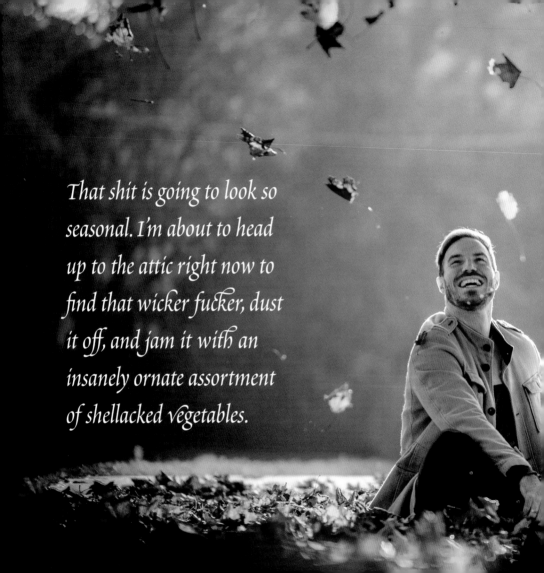

That shit is going to look so seasonal. I'm about to head up to the attic right now to find that wicker fucker, dust it off, and jam it with an insanely ornate assortment of shellacked vegetables.

*When my guests come over
it's gonna be like, BLAMMO!
Check out my shellacked
decorative vegetables, assholes.*

Guess what season it is—
fucking fall. There's a nip in
the air and my house is full
of mutant fucking squash.

I may even throw some multicolored leaves into the mix, all haphazard like a crisp October breeze just blew through and fucked that shit up.

Then I'm going to get to work on making a beautiful fucking gourd necklace for myself. People are going to be like, "Aren't those gourds straining your neck?"

And I'm just going to thread another gourd onto my necklace without breaking their gaze and quietly reply, "It's fall, fuckfaces. You're either ready to reap this freaky-assed harvest or you're not."

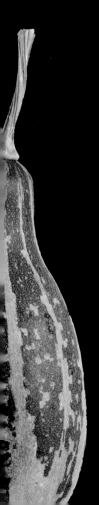

Carving orange pumpkins sounds like a pretty fitting way to ring in the season. You know what else does? Performing an all-gourd reenactment of an episode of DIFF'RENT STROKES— *specifically the one when Arnold and Dudley experience a disturbing brush with sexual molestation.*

Well, this shit just got real, didn't it? Felonies and gourds have one very important commonality: they're both extremely fucking real. Sorry if that's upsetting, but I'm not doing you any favors by shielding you from this anymore.

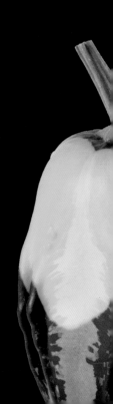

The next thing I'm going to do is carve one of the longer gourds into a perfect replica of the Mayflower as a shout-out to our Pilgrim forefathers.

Then I'm going to do lines of blow off its hull with a hooker. Why? Because it's not summer, it's not winter, and it's not spring.

Grab a calendar and
pull your fucking
heads out of your
asses; it's fall, fuckers.

Have you ever been in an
Italian deli with salamis
hanging from their ceiling?

Well then you're going to fucking love my house. Just look where you're walking or you'll get KO'd by the gauntlet of misshapen, zucchini-descendant bastards swinging from above.

And when you do, you're going to hear a very loud, very stereotypical Italian laugh coming from me. Consider yourself warned.

For now, all I plan to do is to throw on
a flannel shirt, some tattered overalls,
and a floppy fucking hat and stand in
the middle of a cornfield for a few days.
The first crow that tries to land on
me is going to get his avian ass bitch-
slapped all the way back to summer.

Welcome to autumn, fuckheads!

It's rotting decorative gourd
season, motherfuckers.

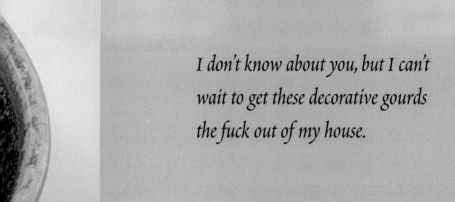

I don't know about you, but I can't wait to get these decorative gourds the fuck out of my house.

The clock expired on these goofy goose-necked bastards about six weeks ago, but I pushed it and the shit got real on me. It's autumn overtime up in here and these fuzzy fuckers need to go. When my guests come over I'm gonna be like, SORRY! My bad on all these rancid ornamental vegetables, you guys. I really should have stayed on top of this perishable shit.

One minute Fall's like, "Hey, check out my delightful fucking harvest, I smell like cinnamon and apples and shit, isn't this nice?" And I'm like, "It's really fucking nice, I wish this could last forever." So Fall's like, "Be careful what you fucking wish for," all ominous and shit. And I'm like, "Take it easy, Fall. Jesus." And Fall's like, "YOU fucking take it easy!"

Next thing I know, I'm rearranging my table horn and my fingers wind up two digits deep in gourd goo. And that shit smells like Fall's crotch after a long jog through a fucking cornfield. And Fall's like, "You like that smell? Huh? Is that the harvest you're lookin' for? Take a good whiff, asshole." And I'm like, "But the shellack . . . it's still so shiny . . ." And Fall just gets up real close on me and whispers, "THE SHELLACK LIES."

I'm about to throw on some kitchen gloves right now and toss these soupy fuckers into a double trash bag so their putrid squash juice doesn't trickle all over my floor on their way out. Then I need to face the music on these Indian corns that went south on me when I wasn't looking. I thought these petrified mini maizes would last forever but their dried-assed niblets took a funky turn and now I've got a foyer-full of foul fucking cobs to unload.

After that, I'm gonna head out to the front steps to do a hazmat sweep on these Jack-O-Lanterns. Seems like yesterday I was carving happy smirks into these adorable dicks. But they've changed now. Mutated into a lazy-eyed mob of shriveled fucking squash zombies with Don King mold fros sprouting out of every hole nature hasn't already shut.

These hay bales in my yard seemed like a nice way to honor the living shit out of Fall. I even stacked them onto an antique wagon and made it rain all over that 1800s asshole with a sack of Red Delicious and some crimson fucking foliage. Turns out I didn't just make a perfect fucking seasonal masterpiece, I made a perfect fucking vermin condo, and those little pricks laid down more miniature bowel movements than I can wrap my head around.

But now I know what I need to do to make this shit right again. I'm gonna make some overdue amends with the harvest gods and gather up every last scrap of Fall I can find, pile it on top of that mouse toilet, then douse it with a nice big can of autumnal gasoline and torch this expired-assed season to kingdom fucking come.

Fall is fucking over,
fuckheads.

Acknowledgments

I'd like thank my agent at WME, Jay Motherfucking Mandel for his sage advice and guidance, my editor at Chronicle, Steve Motherfucking Mockus for his endless positivity and patience, and last but not least, Chris The Mother of all Fuckers Monks, my *McSweeney's* editor who somehow decided to accept this piece and put it out into the world.

About the Author

Colin Nissan is a humor writer, creative director and voice actor who is a frequent contributor to *McSweeney's* and the *New Yorker*, and who has also written for the *New York Times*, the *Paris Review*, and the *Onion*. He lives in Brooklyn.